1598

E·R·I·T·R·E·A

IMAGES OF WAR AND PEACE

GLENYS KINNOCK

E·R·I·T·R·E·A
IMAGES OF WAR AND PEACE

Photographs by Jenny Matthews

Foreword by Basil Davidson

Chatto & Windus
LONDON

Published in 1988 by
Chatto & Windus Ltd
20 Bedford Square
London WC1B 3RP

A CIP catalogue record for this book is available
from the British Library.

ISBN 0 7011 3467 4

Text copyright © Glenys Kinnock
Illustrations copyright © Jenny Matthews

Photoset in Linotron Sabon by
Rowland Phototypesetting Ltd
Bury St Edmunds, Suffolk
Printed in Great Britain by
W. S. Cowell Ltd, Ipswich, Suffolk

The extracts from A FATE WORSE THAN DEBT by
Susan George published by Penguin Books Ltd., and
from THE FOUR HORSEMEN by David Munro,
published by Lyle Stuart, New York, are reproduced by
kind permission of the publishers.

▲▲▲▲ Acknowledgements ▲▲▲▲

This book has been compiled with the invaluable help of James Firebrace and Alison Whyte of War on Want and Alastair Campbell of the *Sunday Mirror*. I am grateful to them for their friendship, their expertise and their commitment. My thanks to Neil for his love and friendship and for always offering encouragement and support, and to Rachel and Steve for their patience and interest.

Thanks too to Sue Nye who so willingly gave up her own time to type all the text and help me to meet a tight deadline.

To War on Want for its unique, humanitarian contribution to long-term development and for giving me the opportunity to visit our programmes in Eritrea.

Thanks most of all to my Eritrean friends for the care they took of us and for their unfailing compassion and humour.

This book is a small tribute to all of them.

▲▲▲▲▲▲▲▲▲ Contents ▲▲▲▲▲▲▲▲▲

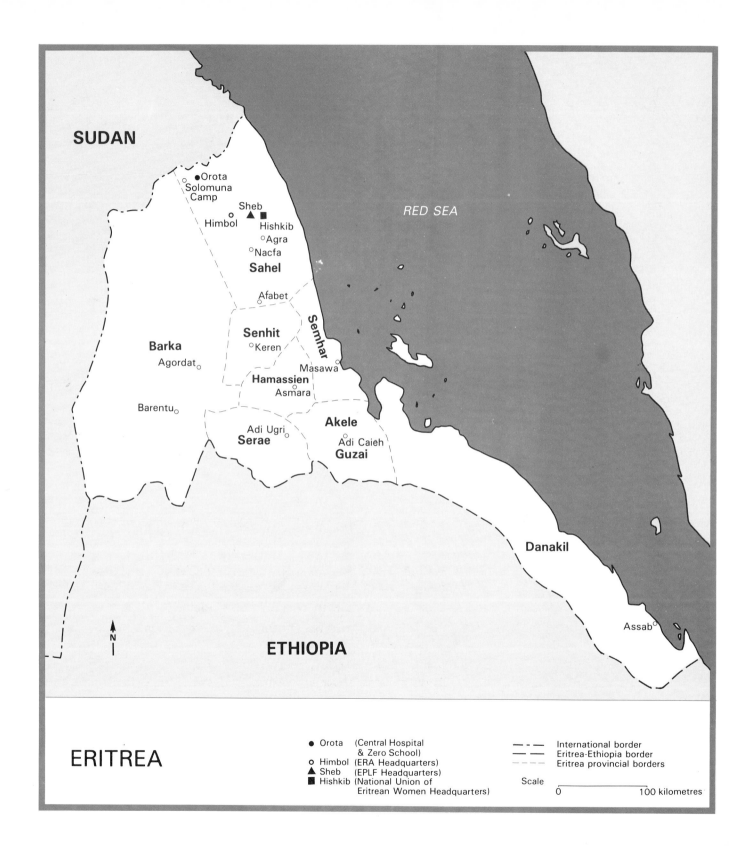

SUDAN

RED SEA

●Orota
○Solomuna
Camp

Sheb ▲■ Hishkib
○Himbol ○Agra
○Nacfa

Sahel

Afabet

Senhit
○Keren

Semhar

Barka
Agordat○

Masawa○

Hamassien
Asmara○

Barentu○

Adi Ugri○

Akele

Serae

Adi Caieh○

Guzai

Danakil

Assab○

N

ETHIOPIA

ERITREA

● Orota (Central Hospital & Zero School)
○ Himbol (ERA Headquarters)
▲ Sheb (EPLF Headquarters)
■ Hishkib (National Union of Eritrean Women Headquarters)

–·–·– International border
– – – Eritrea-Ethiopia border
----- Eritrea provincial borders

Scale
0 ——— 100 kilometres

Eritrea: Basic Facts

Geography

Eritrea covers an area of 124,000 sq km and is approximately the same size as England. It stretches for 1000 km along the Red Sea. To the north and west it is bordered by Sudan, to the south by Ethiopia and to the south-east by Djibouti.

Population

This is estimated at 3.4 million. Fifty per cent of the population is Muslim and fifty per cent is Christian, mainly Coptic. Eighty per cent of Eritreans live in the countryside. Nine languages are spoken.

Political History

1889 Eritrea defined as a nation state under Italian colonisation

1941 Italy defeated in Africa during World War II and Eritrea governed by a British Military Administration

1952 Eritrea federated as an autonomous state with Ethiopia

1952–62 Haile Selassie bans trades unions and political parties

1961 First attacks on police posts and army barracks by the ELF

1962 Haile Selassie annexes Eritrea as Ethiopia's 14th province

1967 First major flight of refugees to Sudan

1970 Eritrean People's Liberation Front formed

1973–4 Famine in Ethiopia contributes to overthrow of Haile Selassie – replaced by Provisional Military Administrative Council, the Derg

1976–8 Liberation movement takes over most of the countryside and towns

1978 Derg breaks ties with USA and allies itself with the Soviet Union

1978–9 'Strategic withdrawal' of EPLF in face of major Ethiopian offensive

1979–82 Five more major offensives in attempt to dislodge EPLF

1982–4 EPLF wins control of south-west and coastal areas

1984 News breaks of famine in Ethiopia and Eritrea. Ethiopian regime refuses offer of cease-fire to allow safe passage of food

1985 Some 80,000 people flee to Sudan in search of food

1987 EPLF breaks through Nacfa Front, the limit of 'strategic withdrawal' in 1978

1988 March: victory of EPLF at Afabet
April: Ethiopian government expels aid agencies from Eritrea and Tigre
May: state of emergency declared by Ethiopian regime
June: EPLF repulses counter offensive of Ethiopian armies

▲▲▲▲▲▲▲▲ Foreword ▲▲▲▲▲▲▲▲

by Basil Davidson

When things go badly it gets hard to believe good news. Quite a lot of people will be thinking this about Europe today. But in Africa, where most things go badly and threaten to get still worse, good news has become extremely hard to believe, and those who bring it have had to learn to be hardily prepared to meet with disbelief. All the same, there *is* good news from Africa, though sometimes hard to find in this continent of an infinite variety of place and people. Whenever it occurs it comes from action at the grass roots of society, action at the base of community, action no longer dependent on stagnant or sterile central governments and their bureaucracies, action derived from democratic forms of mass participation. That kind of action is still scarce in Africa today. But it is becoming less rare.

Eritrea is a small country in the general scale of African countries. It has three or four million people tucked away in mountains and seaward plains at the southern end of the Red Sea. These people have been at war for their anti-colonial liberation for some 27 years; and their imperialist enemy has been and is a savage one. So you would scarcely expect Eritrea to be the kind of place to produce good news. And yet the news from Eritrea brings not only reports of war and its horrendous miseries, it brings hope too. This is because the Eritrean national movement has learned, through many harsh years of difficult self-development, to found its strategy and success in action at and from the grass roots, action precisely concerned with democratic forms of mass participation. That is what this book, essentially, portrays; and that is why the optimism here is soundly based.

You soon find this out as you travel the mountain roads of Eritrea now. Mostly, you travel by night because travel by day would

The poor sorghum crop at Agra showed the effects of drought.

3

expose you to the MIGs and Antonovs of the Ethiopian forces. But night after night, before you and behind you along those hair-raising roads that climb and swerve like spider trails, there are the headlights of heavy trucks carting food from portside in neighbouring Sudan to hungry people in Eritrea, or else returning to fetch more whenever more arrives. These are trucks of the Eritrean Relief Association, part of the Eritrean national movement: early in 1988, when I was there myself, ERA had upward of 200 trucks. Since then, many more have been captured from the armies of the ruling Dergue in Ethiopia and put into service along these roads. Whatever may or may not be happening elsewhere, here is an African people who are seeing to it that food from the outside world, as and when it comes to hand, is going to reach the people who need it. In liberated Eritrea, which now is most of Eritrea, there is a lot of hunger but no famine. And the more food arrives the less hunger there will be.

That might still not be saying a great deal: honest persons, after all, are not so hard to find, even in Africa today. But the food going into Eritrea goes to help a people who have amply proved, over these bitter years, that they also know how to help themselves, and who have shown that none of their afflictions has been able to defeat or demoralise them. They have gone far to heal the wounds of fraticidal strife in their own history. They have continued to wage their anti-colonial war without hatred for Ethiopians who often suffer as much as they do, and who now, with spreading famine, will suffer even more. They have avoided dogmatism. They have set themselves against fanaticism. They have begun to build a peaceful and constructive future.

This excellent book shows some of the evidence. It seems to me to speak for itself: eloquently but also convincingly, for nothing in this

4

Disowned by their country, ignored by the world, Ethiopian prisoners of war taken at the battle of Afabet.

portrayal can be seen to understate the hideous wretchedness of war. On the contrary, the wretchedness of war is seen here for what it is, the governing context within which and against which the Eritreans have to strive despite every conceivable deprivation of a material kind.

But here is a country, as their friend, Amilcar Cabral, used to say of his own, Guinea-Bissau and Cape Verde, where means have been found to bring strength out of weakness, and unity out of conflict. Nothing guarantees the future: Cabral used to say that too. But the Eritrea that this book so poignantly and yet so directly illustrates, and of which Glenys Kinnock writes from her own experience and observation, is a land where the present has become strong with hope and where hope is the child of a sane and shrewd realism.

5

▲▲▲▲▲▲ Introduction ▲▲▲▲▲▲

'Ethiopia, which has been waging a protected war against liberation struggles in its northern provinces (Eritrea and Tigre), is at the bottom of the African poverty barrel. Its GNP is $4.3 billion, which works out to about $110 per Ethiopian, the lowest per capita GNP in the world, according to World Bank figures. This does not prevent Ethiopia from spending $13 per head and per year on its military but only $7 on health and education combined.'

Susan George
A Fate Worse Than Debt

Knowledge is strength. Nomadic women wait for their children's school day to end so that they can get into the 'classroom' for their lessons.

The jeep came to a halt. Our guide pointed at a cluster of acacia and thorn bushes which stood out against an otherwise arid, dull and dusty hillside. There was no sign of life. The guide pressed me to look again and as we clambered over the rocks and boulders we heard soft chanting voices. We moved closer. I saw four rows of people sitting in a classroom built into the hillside and heavily camouflaged to prevent attacks from the air.

That was surprising enough. Even more, the pupils were adults, women of all ages, some with babies on their laps, others with Kalashnikovs resting by their sides. They were learning to count.

The people of Eritrea are at war – a war which they have waged against Ethiopia for twenty-six years. During my visit I learned of an indomitable spirit and a motivation which enables them to fight poverty, famine and a well-armed foe. Yet in the midst of all those contests they do not lose sight of the need to support and encourage women like those I met in the hidden classroom on that first evening.

The members of the Eritrean People's Liberation Front are idealists. But they are also pragmatic and self-critical, never losing sight of the reality of the odds stacked against their fight for independence. Despite a UN resolution, Ethiopia annexed the country in 1962 and ever since the Eritreans have felt abandoned by the international community. Justifiably so. Not one member nation of the UN General Assembly has ever raised the issue of this war which has claimed half a million lives and reduced millions of people to terrible and continual poverty.

Our War on Want team flew to Khartoum on 23 March 1988 on the first stage of a journey which was to take us across Sudan by air and then overland into Eritrea. Basil Davidson was in the Sudanese capital and he talked to us about the Eritrean victory at Afabet which had taken place when he was in Eritrea a week before. It had been a huge and terrible conflict. According to the EPLF, three Ethiopian divisions had been defeated and up to 20,000 Ethiopians had been killed or captured in the battle. In the Western press the coverage had been scanty: in the area itself there were few who would have disagreed with Basil's estimate that the battle of Afabet was the greatest single victory by any liberation army since Dien Bien Phu.

It was against this background that the British Foreign Office showed some anxiety about our safety as we prepared to fly from Khartoum to Port Sudan. I was grateful for this concern, but I must admit we were amused when a British Embassy official explained my position by telling a journalist: 'Mrs Kinnock has no political status' and then added, 'but she does have diplomatic implications'! After much discussion, and on the advice of Basil Davidson who assured us that he had not seen a single Ethiopian warplane during

Diet supplement. High protein food provided by international agencies is an essential part of the effort to improve the physical condition of the Eritrean children.

his visit and that the EPLF would take every possible precaution, we left Khartoum for Port Sudan.

After waiting all day for dusk, and in the care of our EPLF guardian, Naizkhi Kiflu, we left the Red Sea coastal town in two jeeps to begin the fifteen-hour journey into the Eritrean highlands. We marvelled at the skill of our drivers who negotiated tracks that we could not even see and roared across any flat clear spaces like rally drivers. The dusty desert of Sudan gave way to the lunar landscape of Northern Eritrea. In the early morning of 25 March, my 21st wedding anniversary, we arrived at our first EPLF guest

9

house and then waited for the security of dark so that our travels in Eritrea could begin. In the interests of safety no one in Eritrea drives in daylight and people keep close to their camouflaged dwellings.

I was to grow accustomed to surprises during that week and the photographs in this book testify to the resourcefulness, inventiveness and skill of the Eritreans that was manifest everywhere – from the hospital at Orota to the computers in Silicon Valley, and from the scale and standards of Zero School to the light switches dangling from trees which were improvised from used hypodermic syringes. Everything, of course, was to be dominated by discussion of the war – a conflict which for over a quarter of a century has been a terrible diversion of human and material resources from the essential struggle against hunger.

In 1984 and 1985 the images of death in the Horn of Africa filled our television screens and shocked viewers all over the world: supplicant mothers with shrivelled breasts, rows of emaciated corpses shrouded in flimsy cotton wraps, babies crying in agony, desperate people picking up, piece by piece, the grain left on the ground after food distribution.

None of us will ever forget those scenes, or our bewilderment at the fact that the suffering was being brought to us live by satellite and yet no-one seemed to have been able to prevent the catastrophe and international donors seemed unable to respond in time to save the millions suffering famine. Now, as the crises go on, as the drought, the floods, the locusts continue to inflict horror, we ask ourselves what more should be done not just to mitigate the present suffering but to stop it in the future.

Aid – emergency relief and long term support – is essential in the Horn of Africa, as in so many other places. But, by itself, it is not

High class. In the camouflaged hillside school at Solomuna I sat in on the maths lesson with the women – and their babies and their weapons. So many of the messages from Eritrea met in this place.

enough. The truth is that warfare, militarisation and the longest running struggle for independence in black Africa are among the basic causes of the tragedy. Yet the war receives scant attention. The Eritrean–Ethiopian conflict, which played such an important role in the genesis of the famine, has been largely ignored.

The Horn of Africa is, of course, of great strategic importance to the superpowers. The sea lanes of the Red Sea carry about 20 per cent of US oil and about 60 per cent of Western European oil. In addition the fragile politics of the region – both within the Horn and beyond – make the Red Sea an important area of military interest. Since the Second World War the region has been the setting for US–Soviet power games. The Horn of Africa is one place which, for too long, has been the battleground for these geo-political struggles. And, like so many other instances across the poverty ridden regions of the planet, it is yet another place where the poor are the victims in the killing fields. We talk of 40 years of peace, but all over the world the superpowers have continued their proxy wars and millions have perished in the 150 or so local conflicts waged since 1945.

Eritrea, which is in the rough triangle of territory between Ethiopia in the south, Sudan in the west and the long coast of the Red Sea, has long been subject to the will of more powerful states. The area and its people are distinctly different in language, culture and custom from Ethiopia and its inclusion in that state results mainly from a series of historic settlements made largely by external powers, including Britain.

In the 1950s and 1960s the US supported the near-feudal regime of Haile Selassie. When military rule followed a coup in Ethiopia in 1974, the Soviet Union provided arms, advisors and political backing for the Dergue regime, ruled since 1977 by Lt.-Colonel Mengistu Haile Meriam. The leadership in Ethiopia changed; the conflict in Eritrea went on. Now 40,000 EPLF fighters with little more than captured weapons keep some 100,000 Ethiopian soldiers fully engaged. Yet there is a sort of conspiracy of silence in the international community. It seems that a black state annexing a former colony and holding it does not deserve serious attention: the Eritrean–Ethiopian war remains hidden and forgotten. Even during the famine of 1984 and 1985, the fact that 60 per cent of the people in the drought affected areas of Tigre, Wollo and Eritrea were not accessible through Ethiopian Government channels was either overlooked or deliberately obscured.

Political vested interests hold sway and the international community continues even now to turn a blind eye. The International Commission of Jurists puts the Eritrean case very directly:

Body language. One of the Solomuna children who just climbed up for a cuddle. We both enjoyed it. It's better than talking.

12

'Of all the peoples who, since the Second World War, have been the victims of great power rivalries and ambitions, perhaps the one with the greatest claim for consideration is the people of Eritrea. Nevertheless, no nation has yet been willing to raise the issue of the rights of this people in the UN. The truth is that the "Ethiopian question" is a source of embarrassment both to the UN itself and to almost all "interested parties".'

Against this background the rural people of Eritrea continue to struggle to improve their lives. Their aims are not simply nationalistic. Above all they are striving for complete social and economic change. They are neither dogmatic nor fanatical and there are few references to socialist or any other luminaries. It is *their* revolution, uniquely geared to a view of society built on self-reliance and co-operation. 'Model for development' and 'unique experiments' are phrases often heard. But in Eritrea at least they have real meaning. The popular participation of the people is essential to their army and to every other activity. The involvement of women, in a central role with equal rights and responsibilities, is an integral part of the whole process of change.

What I learnt in Eritrea could fill much more than this book. I learnt at first hand that development aid can help build a country's infrastructure and help protect it against the disastrous effects of drought. But responding to crisis won't complete the job; far from it. To do that there must be investment in a partnership which will ensure stability, food security and a real opportunity for people to make their own way and their own future.

▲▲▲▲▲▲▲▲ Solomuna ▲▲▲▲▲▲▲▲

Solomuna, a displaced people's camp, is in a long arid ravine. The first camp was established ten years ago but because of repeated threats to security the people have moved several times.

Now about 8,000 people live in ragged tents built into the sides of the valley. These displaced people are the victims of war and famine. We drank tea sitting on clay seats and talked about the families' experiences and we were told that the Eritrea Relief Association issues rations of flour, lentils and milk powder.

As well as the thousands of displaced people in Eritrea, more than one quarter of the population has fled abroad and it is estimated that as many as one million Eritreans have sought refuge from war and drought in the Sudan alone.

We sang and played at Solomuna with 600 of Eritrea's orphans. Aged 2 to 6, some have seen their fathers bayonetted to death, their mothers raped and butchered. Ebba Hobtom Sium is in charge of the orphanage and many of the people working there were men – all of them loving and affectionate with the children. In fact, all over Eritrea you can see men caring for children almost as frequently as you see women bearing arms.

The children prepared for bed, a blanket laid on a gravel pit, 80 of them packed together under canvas. They clambered all over us and kissed us, fascinated by the earrings and brightly coloured sandals of the women in our party – all in stark contrast to the black plastic footwear worn by the EPLF fighters and just about everyone else. They wanted to know why I had small marbles hanging from my ears and I spent a back breaking session leaning over so that the

School is out. Women leave their evening class and go home to prepare supper.

15

children could feel my earrings and roll them between their fingers. The TV cameras caused great excitement. Hardbitten camera and sound crews, veterans of Beirut and other conflicts across the world, allowed the children to look through the lenses and stroke the furry microphones. They contributed greatly to the excited gaiety at Solomuna that night.

The children are alert and cheerful but clearly in desperate need of parental love and the hugging and touching and kissing which is so much a part of family life. They are the child victims of war, drought and famine. As everywhere, they are the most innocent sufferers. They face an uncertain future fraught with danger from poverty, disease and from the planes which swoop down from the sky. It's worth working to make any contribution towards ensuring that they are the last generation that has to live like this.

Above All the excitement meant that supper was late at Solomuna. As darkness fell the children ate and then sang traditional songs and rhymes. It was the nearest they ever got to sitting still.

Right My earrings – especially the smooth round ones – aroused great interest everywhere. Like all children, the Eritrean girls and boys 'see with their hands'. Touching the earrings was essential.

Above The best camouflage is using what comes naturally.

Right Life is real, life is earnest. Too earnest to go even to classes without a Kalashnikov close to hand.

18

Left Clean, cool water. The joy of getting easily available supplies from the village well instead of trudging for miles and hours to a desert pool is obvious everywhere. For the women especially it leaves time for other work, for education and for the pleasure of just relaxing and having a chat.

Right 'Anyone can do this.' Our BBC and ITN cameramen were a great attraction and they always gave in to the children's appeals to 'have a try'.

▲▲▲▲▲▲ Orota Hospital ▲▲▲▲▲▲

'The casualty figures since the end of World War Two come to about 30 million people, which exceeds the number of Soviet dead, both military and civilian in World War Two, and eventually will exceed the number of all dead in World War Two. So it seems to me that the claim that nuclear weapons have "kept the peace for 40 years" is a complete lie. You cannot call this peace.'

Tom Gervasi
Director, Centre for Military Research

We had been told about the Central Hospital at Orota before we visited it: it was three miles long, built into the mountains and, like everything else in Eritrea, heavily camouflaged against sporadic raids by Ethiopian bomber planes.

It was dark when we pulled up at the entrance. The smell of antiseptic and human flesh hung in the hot night air. There were no driveways, no signposts, no reception lounges. Only dull lights escaping here and there from the underground warren of hospital wards. This was no place for fainthearts. A man whose face had been half blown away was wheeled into the operating theatre where a Dutch surgeon was to perform one of fifteen emergency operations that night. On the floor, young men and women, some in their teens, were waking up to the fact that they had lost limbs or eyesight or had sustained scars that they would bear for the rest of their lives.

Andrew Posman, one of the two Dutch doctors working as volunteers, spoke admiringly of the quality of care being provided by the Eritrean doctors and of the courage of his patients. He told

'I'll be back.' EPLF fighters recover, with smiles, among gravestones.

23

us: 'One young man came in with his face blasted off. He has been in about six times for treatment. When he woke up, his first question was "When can I go back to the front line?"'

Despite the grim sight of people with ghastly injuries lying on stretchers under trees, the techniques perfected by the Eritrean medical team in plastic surgery are outstanding. An experienced surgeon himself, Dr Posman said that doctors in the West could learn a lot from some of the methods being practised at Orota, particularly in plastic surgery, as so many patients need emergency treatment for facial and other external injuries.

I had a dreadful experience as I left the hospital. I stepped back in the darkness on to the body of a young and very sick wounded woman soldier lying on a stretcher in the corridor. She was unconscious and didn't know what I'd done. I did. It will always haunt me.

A visit to the mother and baby unit provided a happier note to our visit that night. The midwife on duty, like so many people in Eritrea, spoke good English. She was keen to show us the pride and joy of the maternity ward – a new ultrasound scanner, donated by the Swedes, which meant that the best in new technology could now be combined with natural childbirth methods.

We returned the following day to visit the pharmaceutical laboratory funded by War on Want and to see the other wards. The Central Hospital has nine units – orthopaedic, chest and cardio-vascular, neurological, plastic surgery, opthalmic, gynaecological, internal and physiotherapy. It moved to its present location in 1982. The previous, much smaller site had been bombed.

It was on that second day that I witnessed one of the most indelible scenes of our visit. A small man, Mehemse Alemse, 26 years old and one of the Ethiopian POWs among about 1,500

Hospital queue. All the available beds are filled with more urgent cases so these EPLF fighters wait for treatment to their wounds outside Orota hospital.

24

Eritrean patients at the hospital, was standing near us. Wounded in the chest and in a state of shock, he was being comforted by Simon Haile, an Eritrean doctor, who gently placed his arm around the other man's shoulder. When he felt better, Mehemse wandered off to look after an Eritrean who was in pain. This moving episode brought home to all of us the futility of war and the humanity of people. Young Ethiopian men, drafted into the army, are fighting a war they do not want to fight; they are unable to return home. The considerate attitude of the Eritreans towards them amazes and inspires. Dr Simon gave a resigned smile as he said 'This is a very stupid war.'

All of the people we met at the hospital – doctors, nurses, surgeons, working round the clock, many of them separated from their own families – were receiving no salary. Everyone taking part in the struggle in Eritrea is called a 'fighter'.

Left The post-operative ward at Orota Hospital.

Right The cost of war. EPLF fighters – a woman and a man – recover from major surgery on wounds inflicted during the battle of Afabet. Both had terrible chest wounds but these stretchers were the only resting place available.

27

Every 'fighter' works simply for his or her food and basic clothing. No one complains. Nor is there any trace of deeper resentments. Daniel, our driver throughout the visit, was a lad of about nineteen. He was always with us, and often when we arrived at our destination at some late hour would wrap himself up in his blanket and have forty winks in the front of the jeep. He always seemed to wake up just as we emerged from some camouflaged doorway and was ready to start the engine. One day I asked him how he managed with so little sleep. He laughed; 'I'll sleep when the war is over.'

We swapped our dusty trainers for plastic flipflops, piled up at the doorway of the pharmacy. It was 2 am, but the pharmacists, all in blue coats and hats, were beavering away as if it were the middle of a working day. This was a real high point for the War on Want team. Our organisation helps to fund the laboratory which bypasses multinational drug companies to produce no less than 40 per cent of the Eritrean's basic drugs requirements and saves precious funds.

In the tablet section the standard of production was sophisticated and the pace was fierce. Fifty million tablets of 32 varieties are manufactured there every year. Antibiotics, anti-malarial tablets, aspirin, paracetamol, vitamins and tablets to treat intestinal infections are made. An important part of the pharmaceutical production is the making up of intravenous fluid packs, expensive to import from the Sudan because of their bulk. Since 1987 the pharmacists have been producing capsules and there are plans to introduce injectibles and ointments as well.

As we wandered around the sterile rooms, we went into one which looked at first glance to be filled with steel office furniture of the kind seen in the more modernistic of executive suites. On closer

Doing really good. The War on Want team were specially proud of the drug protection unit at Orota because we are directly involved in funding the project that provides 40% of Eritrea's drugs and medicines.

28

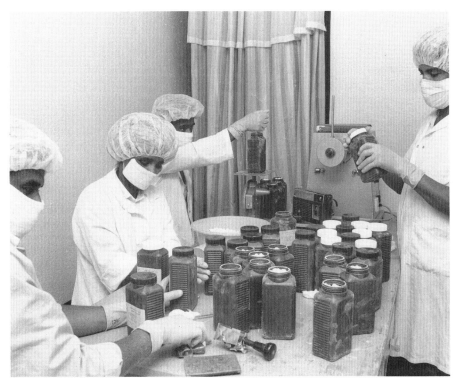

The men's 'ward' at Orota hospital.

inspection the cabinets in which tablets and other items were stored proved to be made of old ammunition boxes. Swords into plough-shares indeed, and showing the same resourcefulness which we had seen everywhere: old shells made into kitchen pots and pans, cannibalised armour into furniture; the ubiquitous black rubber sandals made from tyres, the disused medical syringes hanging from trees. 'Everything', say the Eritreans, 'has its use – and then another use.'

The pattern of ill-health in Eritrea is typical of a poor Third World country. Death and disease have been aggravated by the years of drought and famine and damage from the war, but most health problems stem from low standards of nutrition, a contamin-ated and inadequate water supply, poor sanitation and housing. Malnutrition and anaemia are widespread, lowering people's resist-ance to infectious diseases. Malaria, tuberculosis, respiratory infec-tions and intestinal parasites are endemic. In the lowland areas, nomadic women and children sleep in tents while men sleep outside where they are susceptible to malarial mosquitoes.

The EPLF started a health service in 1970 with a single mobile health clinic, only able to give basic first aid. Training of the first barefoot doctors began in 1972 but it was not until 1975 that the health service really started to develop when hundreds of Eritrean doctors, nurses and paramedical staff fled the towns and joined the EPLF. The real battle was raging south of Nacfa, 60 miles away, but the front line was also here at Orota Hospital, where doctors and nurses worked through the night and where young men and women fought for their lives.

Man's humanity to man. An Ethiopian prisoner of war tends a wounded EPLF fighter. Why did it take wounds to bring these two men together?

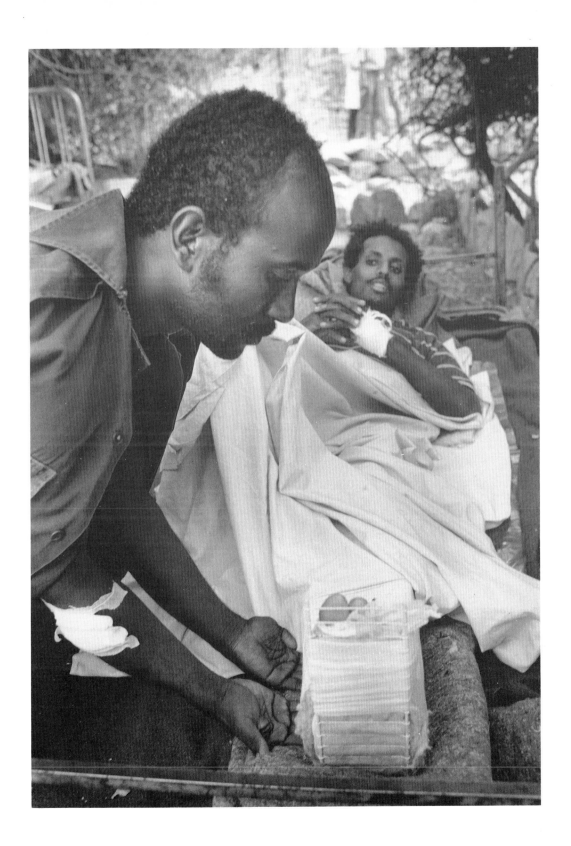

▲▲▲▲▲▲▲ Zero School ▲▲▲▲▲▲▲

According to Wolde Giorgis Andeberhan, Regional Director of Eritrean Education, the Eritreans are not interested in disseminating political theory or ideology in the classrooms at Zero school. The school is far more concerned with maintaining academic standards and the children's cultural and national identities.

When we visited the school the 4,000 children had just heard of the Eritrean victory at Afabet; many of their faces were clouded with concern when they talked about it, not knowing if their own parents were safe or not. As you spot the anti-aircraft guns on the hilltops you cannot for a second forget that you are in a country at war. We were told of the bombing raid on the school in 1984 when three children were killed, and how MIGs had flown over the school two days before our visit. We saw the dark, dank underground dormitory where 80 children slept at night.

The school is carefully concealed. It is the largest school I have ever visited and consists of several age groupings in units dotted along a 12 kilometre valley. When we had our obligatory cup of tea before visiting the children and teachers at work, I looked around wondering where the school could actually be. How was it possible to completely conceal anything containing 4,000 people, let alone lively children?

Zero School is the proud centrepiece of liberated Eritrea's new educational system. Chemistry, history, English, maths, sport, music and the two main languages, Tigrinya and Tigre, are taught in classrooms made of sticks and foliage or under rocks or near to ditches and slit trenches where the pupils can run for shelter if they hear the sound of aircraft.

A camouflaged classroom at Zero School.

We chanced upon a 14-year-old girl who had left the high schools, hamburgers, teenage fashions and freeways of the USA for a stone seat and a desk-top made from a wrecked tank in a classroom made of trees in Eritrea. Five months before I met her, Awet Tekeste lived in Los Angeles. Then her mother decided to return to her Eritrean home to fight. She joined the front line troops of the EPLF, one third of whom are women.

The young girl said, 'I don't miss much really, maybe Coke and ice cream, but I am happy to be with my people. If my mother dies, it is because the war has to be fought. I am not scared for her.' It was a chilling sentiment to hear from any child but, spoken with quiet certainty in a Californian accent, it had a tone of matter of fact confidence that somehow avoided being unfeeling.

Like all the other girls at Zero School, Awet has equal opportunity with the boys and is especially encouraged to be interested in subject areas which are more traditionally reserved for them. 'Engineer, scientist, doctor, teacher are words that don't have a sex, aren't they?' one of the EPLF women said.

The teachers are not paid and they are intent on teaching a co-operative, non-competitive approach. The children are encouraged to value and respect one another and to strive to achieve their full potential whatever it might be. This approach is fundamental to the whole philosophy of the EPLF and the fulfilment of each individual is seen as necessary to the future wellbeing of the country. It is remarkable that, when resources are so scarce, they are prepared to devote so much to literacy and education, but they regard both as the keys to individual and collective advance and commit what pitiful means they have to that end.

I saw a grave shortage of books and equipment and I marvelled at

High School drop in. Awet Tekeste exchanged a Los Angeles High School for an Eritrean desert school when her mother came home.

36

young people and their teachers being able to cope with one book between six of them. It was at Zero School that we were able to meet up with Paul Highfield from Lancashire who has spent seven years teaching Eritrean children. He is deeply attached to their cause and calls the EPLF 'a government in exile'. I admired the devotion to learning shown by his pupils. He told us that nothing would keep them away from the classroom and they all looked forward to the time when they could contribute to their country's independence. The views of the children themselves testified to the fact that this was no high-minded sentiment but a practical fact of life for them.

Above The children at Zero School have learnt to cultivate their own fresh vegetables.

Right A war veteran turned biology teacher.

The splendid finale to our day was a performance of traditional singing and dancing given by the children. We saw a marvellous display which represented the nine nationalities of Eritrea, and the band blew their way gustily through a medley including Lennon and McCartney, Bob Dylan and George Gershwin on cornets and trombones donated by Italians of Eritrean origin. We had been greeted by an unforgettably upbeat Eritrean version of 'Let It Be', yet my attempts to have a conversation about the Beatles were a complete flop – the youngsters had never heard of them!

I felt 'at home' at the school and was impressed by the evident mutual respect between the students and between the students and their teachers. There is no place in the school for punishment, sanctions or imposed discipline – a far cry from our own experience, I fear. And if it sounds idyllic, it certainly wasn't. The place, the conditions, the war forbid that. But as an experienced teacher, I have to say that even in the many good schools that I know, I've never seen teacher–pupil relationships like those I saw among the sticks and stones of Zero School.

Above The Eritrean journey had many musical moments and memories but the Beatles and jazz at Zero School certainly made an impression. The quintet, with the Horn of Africa sounds, blows cool.

Right War makes useful junk. An ammunition box converted into a satchel.

40

▲▲▲▲▲▲▲▲▲▲ War ▲▲▲▲▲▲▲▲▲▲

'The world does not have to fight wars. It is not a necessary function of our species. There are alternative ways of reaching solutions to problems, but the current system in many cases precludes them. Politicians and generals may start wars, but people have to fight them. People who don't talk like us or look like us or share exactly the same political view are not the enemy. Not the Russians, or the Mozambicans, not the Palestinians or the Eritreans, not the Vietnamese or the Nicaraguans, none of them is the enemy. War is.'

David Munro
The Four Horsemen

Four years have passed since Bekele Bulto saw his wife and five children. He was a doctor in Addis Ababa when he was pressganged into joining the Ethiopian Army. One day he was looking after the sick, a job he was well qualified for: the next, he was heading for the front line of the war with Eritrea. He was captured on his first day of combat. I find it impossible to put into words the grief in this handsome man's eyes. They were quite simply the saddest eyes I've ever seen. 'My eldest will be 26 now' he told me, 'and the youngest 14.' Does he expect to see them again? He stares at the ground and shrugs his shoulders.

'Home' is now Orota prisoner of war camp. Several thousand Ethiopians are watched over by a small number of Eritreans. Nobody tries to escape. There is nowhere to go in the wilderness and, in any case, they are prisoners terrified of being freed.

The day before I went to the camp, EPLF General Secretary

Army vehicles destroyed by the Eritreans. Anything which could be salvaged was gathered up for a future use.

43

Isseyas Afeworki had told us that, in the wake of the battle for Afabet, they planned to release thousands of their Ethiopian prisoners. 'They cost us too much in food and clothing', he said. I thought that we would be pleasing the men at Orota in giving them this news. I was wrong. 'I won't go back while we have the same rulers,' said Lemme Legesse, aged 34 and the father of two children, aged seven and fourteen. A prisoner for four years, he feared he would be shot as a deserter, jailed or sent straight back to the frontline if he returned home. 'I won't go back. They have no justice,' he said.

Seble Barente, captive for 8 years, said 'I am better off here. At least they feed us. In Ethiopia, while we fight the wars, there is no money to feed our children.'

Bekele Bulto, aged 50, now teaches English to fellow prisoners. It struck us as a terrible waste of a man trained and skilled as a doctor. 'I feel angry, yes, but above all sad,' he said, again and again.

The depression and anguish of these men stems not just from the stunted lives they lead but from their own government's denial that they even exist. They say that they were sent to war ill-prepared and ill-informed. Their training was almost non-existent and they believed the government line that the EPLF were merely a small bunch of 'bandits'. At the EPLF camps they are fed and clothed and left alone to live out the endless days of captivity. Many say they are treated better by their captors than by their own government. Certainly they looked fit; the condition of thousands of POWs couldn't have been specially created to impress us on our visit. The Ethiopians send them to war where they obey orders, get captured and, to all intents and purposes, cease to exist. It is cynicism on an unbelievable scale. In reaction, some of the captured Ethiopians have joined the EPLF to fight.

The tireless, pointless football games take place every afternoon. The prisoners are healthy and well cared for but the feeling of hopeless boredom lies over everyone. These men are losing the best years of their lives.

44

Good to be alive – even as a prisoner.

Orota was the third prison camp we visited and by far the biggest. The routine is never changing – eat, football, classes, eat, lounge around aimlessly, sleep.

Elsewhere in Eritrea, in makeshift camps around Afabet, thousands more prisoners, still dazed and confused by battle, were waiting to be shipped to a permanent camp. 'We can't understand why we're here, why we're fighting this war,' said Mengiste Alemna. He said he was unsure, before he left for the front line, of the scale of the war. 'We didn't know people were prisoners of war. We thought there was a little skirmish with a small number of bandits, that's all.'

Mengiste Bontoche, aged 27 and a regular soldier for seven years, said, 'We'll be shot if we go back. They don't want people to go back because we could tell others the truth about this war – so we'd be treated as deserters.'

His guards claimed that, even after Afabet had been lost, Ethiopian radio was broadcasting results of football matches in the area which had never taken place. In Ethiopia as elsewhere, the medium is the message. In a country where control over communication is complete, the fiction that the war against the EPLF is 'a little skirmish' can be sustained.

Regrettably, the International Red Cross, while giving help where it can with food and blankets, is limited in its ability to support these men in the prisoner of war camps. For all official purposes Eritrea has not been regarded formally as a country for decades, but is seen as a province of Ethiopia. Technically war has never been declared and, since the Red Cross cannot get the Ethiopian prisoners recognised as prisoners of war, the captured men and casualties do not therefore exist. Bekele Bulto, Lemme Legesse and

Safe keeping. Security at the POW camp was certainly strict. The Ethiopian prisoners simply have nowhere to go.

48

tens of thousands like them are the forgotten men of a forgotten war, abandoned by their government, fighting in a conflict ignored by the world.

The journalists with us went to the battlefront at Afabet and rejoined our group a day later. Alastair Campbell described the scene:

'The Eritrean fighters were lazing around in the sun, laughing. A motley looking bunch in khaki shirts, denim jeans and rubber sandals, they had just overwhelmed Ethiopian armour, artillery and infantry and taken Afabet. It was one of the biggest battles in the history of the war with Ethiopia. They had ripped down the pictures of Mengistu and other eminences which had adorned the wall behind them and now they were poring over the sacks of literature

The deserted Ethiopian stronghold at Afabet after the battle. The slogan reads 'Let international proletarianism flourish!'

50

left by the Ethiopians as they fled the Regional Army Headquarters, stopping only to listen to the B B C World Service account of the battle they'd just won.

'Basil Davidson, who was with the E P L F around the time of the Afabet rout, had filed a report to the B B C. The morale of those listening was ecstatic.

'They were laughing at a yellow guidebook which, they explained, was given by the Ethiopians to their frontline troops, telling them how to deal with the "bandits" of the E P L F. Thirty-nine-year-old Esey Shiker Abraham, a fighter for 13 years, read aloud in a solemn announcer's voice: "They are weak, confused, low in number. They are helped by Arabs, and imperialists but their leaders are weak and driven by personal greed and ambition." By now, Abraham had reduced his fellow fighters to tears of laughter. The best was yet to come: "When you point a gun at them, they run away." The place erupted.

'Nearby, in an overcrowded green shed, hundreds of Ethiopian soldiers were captive. "Try telling all that to them" said Seyoum Guiwet.'

According to the EPLF, three entire divisions and a mechanised brigade had been put out of action – that means 18,000 troops killed, captured or forced to flee. Around 50 tanks were captured, along with several dozen trucks and 60 pieces of artillery. Hidden in the countryside, being repaired or checked for battle worthiness, were Stalin Organ multiple rocket launchers, T-55 tanks, 130 millimetre howitzers, all of them 'liberated' – as the fighters called it – from the Ethiopians. Three Soviet officers working with the

Spoils of war. The captured rocket launcher is – like everything else in Eritrea – carefully camouflaged. It was amongst the huge amount of armour and artillery taken at Afabet.

Overleaf War makes re-usable junk.

Ethiopian Army as military advisors were also taken prisoner.

Had the battle of Afabet taken place anywhere with a large media congregation, the loss of life and the scale of the fighting would have inspired worldwide interest and demands for action to stop the war. Had it not been for Basil Davidson's presence and the fact that TV crews covering my own visit managed to obtain EPLF film of the fighting, such a tragic waste of human life would have attracted little reporting.

Even 10 days after the fighting, the British TV crew's film captured something of the scale of the battle. On the drive to Afabet, the press party told me, an apparently never ending stream of Ethiopian trucks was coming the other way from the battlefield. Some were piled high with ammunition. Others were towing weaponry. Further on, the reporters found the perfect spot – at least in television terms – from which to file their reports. They were at the foot of the mountain from where the first EPLF shot had been fired. Burnt out tanks stretched as far as the eye could see; guns and bodies so badly burned they barely resembled corpses littered the roadside; the remains of Ethiopian truck drivers could be seen hanging out of windows, burnt to death as they attempted to flee. It was a place of horror and slaughter from which the world could be told about the war by television.

The Eritreans, resourceful as ever, were combing every inch of the battlefield, looking for tools, bullets, tyres, even used shell cases, anything that might be useful to them.

It is little wonder the EPLF fighters were so overjoyed at their victory. Afabet, as well as being the regional Army HQ for Colonel Mengistu's troops, housed the crack 'Nadaw' division. The name means 'destroy'. The EPLF delighted in telling us that they were the

Plastic sandals, khaki drabs and a light machine gun – full battle dress for an EPLF woman fighter.

ones who had done the destroying. Taking into account the poverty, the shattered economy, the scavenged weapons and equipment and the negligible infrastructure of Eritrea, it was clearly a significant victory. The EPLF are fighting against the biggest army in black Africa with air and logistical support, and they are not losing.

First the Americans, and then the Russians, have poured billions of dollars in military aid into Ethiopia, whereas the EPLF has had to rely on its resourcefulness, its captured weaponry and its unity. That last strength, unity, should not be underestimated. Many of the Ethiopians we spoke to admitted, said they believed, they were in the wrong in attempting to hang on to Eritrea.

I saw no such doubt in any Eritrean I met. They have learned bitter lessons from the divisions of past years. Whether talking with nurses, teachers, fighters, the old who had never left their homeland, the young graduates who had returned from universities across the world, I found their dedication to their cause and their commitment to victory is total. This despite a death toll for the conflict that some estimates put as high as 141,000 Eritreans and 40,000 Ethiopians.

Wherever we travelled there was no escaping the conflict: the living with camouflage as a fact of life; the daytime restrictions on travel because of fear of attack by the Soviet MIG 23 fighter bombers; the number of tanks and artillery; the limbless ex-fighters. The phrase 'total war' kept occurring to me with a strength of meaning it had never had before.

The EPLF may be a more formidable force than the Ethiopians tell their troops it is. But, in the end, it will be politics, negotiation, agreement that will decide when the killing can stop and the rebuilding of this war-shattered land can begin. Meanwhile, the orphans, the POWs and the starving are just the pawns.

War artist sketching during a MIG attack.

Above Victory is sweet. EPLF fighters listen to reports of their triumph on the BBC World Service. Ethiopian soldiers had been told that these men were disorganised bandits who would run away. In reality they inflicted complete defeat on a whole army corps with tanks and artillery, with little more than small arms and a great deal of cunning.

Right End of the war. Exhausted Ethiopian prisoners of war wait for dispatch to the camps – and years more waiting to return to their homes.

▲▲▲▲▲▲▲▲▲▲ Agra ▲▲▲▲▲▲▲▲▲▲

After the usual overnight drive, complete with bumps and groans, hyenas and Daniel the driver's taped Eritrean music (a unique cross between Arab sounds and Reggae played by half a brass band with a rock'n'roll rhythm section), we arrived at Agra where we were to look at an agricultural project involving the nomadic people of that area. This is part of the work of the Eritrea Consortium of voluntary aid organisations of which War on Want is the lead agency. All the agricultural tools for the Agra Project have been provided by the Consortium.

Agra was at the end of our visit to Eritrea and I had had a particularly difficult night – as far as mice were concerned, that is. I have always recognised my fear of mice to be completely irrational and in Eritrea, surrounded by all the evidence of human struggles against misery and danger, I was more than usually disgusted with my weakness. I made every effort of will to throw off my ludicrous dread of these tiny and harmless animals. I failed – so providing an endless source of hilarious amusement for the party with me and the Eritreans as they mounted what came to be known as 'the mouse patrols'. Even fear seems to have its uses.

Alison Whyte, War on Want's Press Officer, welcomed the diversion since, as she said, it took her mind off her charges in the press group. It provided everyone with limitless stories of the strategies adopted to ensure that I did not see mice running over my pillows or into my suitcase.

At a stop on the way to Agra on that last day I saw several of these creatures and was forced to conduct – or try to conduct – a serious conversation crouched on the top of a desk. At night, as we grabbed a few hours sleep, I knew that each camouflaged roof was infested with mice. When Alison and I lay down on our stone beds at night

Nomadic women at Agra.

I longed for the three hours to end so that I could sleep in the safety of the bouncing jeep.

Agra is a long, broad desert valley peopled by nomads who grapple with a harsh and cruel environment with an expertise born of experience. One hundred and fifty families have been given their own plot of land by the EPLF and they are able to grow vegetables and grain. But here, as everywhere else, everything is heavily camouflaged to prevent targetting by Ethiopian MIGS.

It was 06.30 and school had just begun with an exercise class. A class of young children sprinted around in obedience to their teacher's whistle. 'Arms up, arms down, legs together, legs astride': the children swung and jumped in the rhythm familiar everywhere. It could have been a playground anywhere in the world, but this was a sandy space beneath towering cliffs; the exercises have to finish before the planes arrive from Ethiopia on their morning patrol.

Here, I think, I was most aware of the cultural difference between ourselves and the people of Eritrea. We talked, however, with ease using a three-way translation between Tigrinya, Tigre and English.

James Firebrace, Programme Officer for War on Want, was especially keen that we should see the well in the village and the pump which had been funded by the Eritrea Consortium. James has a particular passion for water projects and will talk at great length and with even greater knowledge about rigs, bore holes and drills. There are few experiences more heartening, however, than seeing War on Want's fund-raising efforts showing such great results: the women collected clean water from a well near their homes, making exhausting 10 mile treks a thing of the past. The drilling rig has made fresh water flow across a wide area of Eritrea and the

'Getting down to it.' Children line up for class at Agra school with the same mixture of eagerness and reluctance, shuffling and chatting as are shown at the beginning of the school day everywhere.

Overleaf The dawn exercise class. The children spend the rest of the daylight hours close to cover because of the danger of air attacks.

64

agricultural scheme in Agra captures water from the hills and irrigates crops for the settled nomadic community.

I met with the village assembly and representatives of women and other workers. Then we sat in a circle near the well with the women in their vibrantly coloured clothes. They were articulate and confident. They greeted us with the very direct question, 'What is your business here?' and then, in conversation, proudly proclaimed that they no longer served their husbands food under the flap of the tent. Now they could look them in the face and indeed, as they reported with peals of laughter, their husbands often served them with tea.

These Muslim women felt valued; they had land of their own for the first time and they were excited by the prospects they had been offered. Now they read their own letters, they speak out in assembly meetings and, because of greater understanding and education, they have been able to improve their own lives and the lives of their families. It was clear to me that the literacy achieved in the makeshift classrooms or under the trees has also brought a political insight and confidence previously denied to women like them.

Of course there are many traditional practices against which the EPLF campaign. Circumcision and infibulation, the dowry system and arranged marriages still exist but a careful and persuasive education programme is taking place.

I learned from these women how much it meant to them to learn to read or write. Small babies settled down for a rest and a little light refreshment as mothers had a geography lesson.

Left Beauty.

Above A barefoot midwife at Agra demonstrates her skills.

Right The midwife feeds her own twins.

Food and water, the essentials
of daily life.

▲▲▲▲▲ Askalu Menkarios ▲▲▲▲▲

No account of a visit to Eritrea would be complete without a description of the work of the National Union of Eritrean Women.

The role of women and their active participation play an important part in discussions and decisions in Eritrea and the EPLF has done a great deal to change the situation of Eritrean women. The people of the EPLF are, however, the first to acknowledge that there is much to be done in their land where the women still bear the greatest burden of domestic and agricultural work. Hard work, poverty, malnutrition and repeated pregnancies continue to take their toll of health and life.

Eritrean mothers make huge sacrifices. Many spend 10 to 12 hours a day working with the EPLF in schools, in the health service and at the battle lines. This does not mean that they love their children any less, but their commitment to the cause makes great demands and the children I met who were old enough to discuss the matter made it clear that they understand that. Frequently this pattern of living means that mothers give a great deal of time to looking after each other's children. It produces a strong sense of confidence for the mothers and security for the children.

Mother of two, Askalu Menkarios, head of the National Union of Eritrean Women, said to me, 'When I am away from my babies I am not worried. They are cared for by other men and women in the EPLF. My babies need me and I give them love, but I don't see in terms of only my children. There are thousands of babies I have to work for.'

I saw at Orota hospital the young female combatants who had been wounded by bullets and shrapnel at Afabet. EPLF women command tanks and hold high rank in the army. They make up one third of the forces at the front.

Askalu Menkarios, head of the National Union of Eritrean Women.

Isseyas Afeworki was clear about the importance of recognising women in the EPLF's work. With a twinkle in his eye, he asserted that 'It would be stupid to ignore such a formidable force – Eritrea will never be liberated without 50 per cent of the population.'

The radical social and economic programmes which are being implemented include women at all levels. The services which are provided take their special needs and the difficulties they have in taking up new opportunities in health or education into account. One remarkable contribution which the EPLF makes to womens' lives, for instance, is to produce and distribute sanitary towels – a commonplace necessity that is not always a priority product in developing countries.

> 'We have confident and courageous women who know that they do not belong in the kitchen. They can do more than have children – they can do everything and anything which society needs.
>
> 'We have 80–90 per cent illiteracy, so there is much to do. You see, we have made change, but this is only the beginning. It is a long process. We have been successful in converting many women in many places but it is a long term struggle.'

This is the philosophy behind much of what we saw in Eritrea. They take a long-term view and are able to articulate a vision that goes beyond the war and its terrifying repercussions, and provide opportunities that have the most practical effects of meeting immediate needs, and of laying foundations for development.

I met women who had been on courses which taught them about

75

the use of farm implements, crop trials and the conservation of natural resources. At Silicon Valley I saw women working alongside men as watch repairers, mechanics, radio operators and electronic experts.

Askalu explained: 'It is not easy to call women to a meeting, talk to them, and teach them about what their role should be. It is not easy to provide literacy classes and political education. Most of all it is not easy for them.'

Hearing Askalu say this in a confident and reasoned voice, and seeing myself the evidence of such co-operation and change everywhere, I understood the force that her words had for the future.

The young mothers, with babes in arms, eventually walked away from our discussion and waited under the trees for the children to vacate the classrooms so that they could begin their own lessons. There is a real sense of urgency about their wish to become literate, to be able to learn alongside their children. For them it is the essence of liberation.

At the mealtime at midday we were taken to a hilltop where, with typical generosity, the villagers had killed a goat in our honour. The barefoot midwife with us sat chatting and suckling her own twins. Like all the other barefoot midwives, nurses and doctors, she treks from village to village to care for her patients and teach basic health care and nutrition. She told me with immense professional pride that, of the 200 mothers in her care during the last year, not one had died in childbirth and all their babies are alive. The contrast with conditions in the past was clear – three of her own babies had died in the years before the present rudimentary but highly effective maternity care had been brought to the area.

Later in the day we saw the children line up for their sup-

All even. Equality of the sexes in the EPLF extends, of course, to the army. Women serve in all ranks, including Battalion Commander.

plementary feeding – the extra nourishment they need to build up their frail bodies. Older children stirred the foaming high protein drink mixture which the younger ones drank with obvious relish.

Then there was time for a quick game of football with a couple of journalists who experienced obvious difficulties with the ball of rags used by the children. There and then we decided to appeal for footballs for these youngsters and, thanks to the generosity of *Sunday Mirror* readers and British football clubs, we have been able to collect hundreds of the genuine leather articles for use by the budding champions in the Eritrean desert. If they show the skills with the leather balls that they learned with the bundles of rags, we'll be hearing more of them.

Now it was time to wait for the dark and the long journey back to the guesthouse. We spent the time talking about our day and looking forward to the inevitable but delicious pasta – made possible by the fact that Italian settlers had abandoned their spaghetti machines when they left.

▲▲▲▲▲▲ Isseyas Afeworki ▲▲▲▲▲▲

Isseyas Afeworki, Secretary
General of EPLF.

EPLF Secretary General Isseyas Afeworki is a tall, lean man with a modest, shy manner. His toughness, resilience and determination are as much a natural part of him as his quiet, precise voice. The EPLF fighters regard him with deep affection. He came to meet us at the guesthouse at Sheib and we had a long talk over endless cups of tea about the long-term effects of the Afabet victory and the capture of the Russian military advisors.

When I asked for his view of the relationship between Mengistu and Gorbachev he replied, 'It is not a new policy coming from Moscow that says that the situation must change. The *reality* of their involvement here is a good lesson for them. They know that this war has been lost – 10 years of fighting and it has not brought any political or military advantage to the government of Mengistu and now the Russians realise it.'

He was confident about the future. He told us with complete calm and assurance, 'We have reached a point of no return, there will never be any going back. Now we look forward to the time when the outside world comes in at last with a real contribution to peace.'

The general reports we'd heard about Isseyas Afeworki had been of a rather solemn, ascetic man. He proved, however, to have an endearing sense of humour and when our party went for dinner at his 'base' in a mountain canyon we were able to have a relaxed, warm and friendly evening. It was unintentionally enlivened by the Eritrean 'official photographer'. Seeking a vantage point from which to take a shot of us eating our spaghetti (photographers are the same the world over), he lost his balance and, with a despairing yell, fell out of the tree outside the guesthouse. Fortunately, neither he nor the camera was hurt. It was something our guides never allowed the unfortunate man to live down as he followed us around.

▲▲▲▲▲▲▲▲ Conclusion ▲▲▲▲▲▲▲▲

*'Europe is a prepared battlefield. So the worry of the
Europeans is that if there was a conflict somewhere in the
Third World it would unleash a major war which would take
place in Europe. I think it is in the particular interest of
Europe to work for peaceful solutions to the problems in the
Third World.'*

Olof Palme
Prime Minister of Sweden, 1982–86

The Eritrean Relief Association confirmed that the economic and
food situation in the area gives cause for serious concern and that
the people always live on a knife-edge. Apart from the fragility of
life in any land that is mainly arid and subject to locusts, floods and
regional droughts, they always have to take into account the war,
the bombings, the continuous movement of displaced persons, and
all of the resulting costs and disruptions.

Lasting peace and security can and must be achieved. In Eritrea
we see a highly motivated and disciplined liberation movement and
a demoralised Ethiopian army. There are signs that there are
elements within the Ethiopian Politburo who favour a negotiated
settlement. It has to be hoped that the UN, the OAU and others will
take an interest and that world leaders will realise their clear and
moral obligation.

The Eritreans feel isolated and abandoned but still they press for a
UN controlled plebiscite as the only solution. They know that whatever military success they gain, the strife will only be permanently
ended with a vote to show the popular will, not by violence alone.

Ironically – and despite the barren nature of much of the area –
Eritrea would be a net exporter of food and, according to a recent

Serious stuff. After lots of
laughing and teasing the class
monitor eventually adopted a
suitably earnest pose for the
camera.

81

report, could be 'a potential bread basket for the neighbouring African and Arab markets'. But during a quarter of a century of war and even during the years of good rainfall, Eritrea has rarely even met 20 per cent of the food needs of its people.

Perhaps the greatest hope now lies with President Gorbachev and his strategy for ending regional conflicts. Moscow seems to have lost its enthusiasm for pumping unlimited money and arms into an army whose morale is battered and whose use seems to lack any real strategic or tactical purpose. When the Ethiopian leader visited Moscow in 1987 Mikhail Gorbachev cautioned him 'to proceed from realities and not outrun stages of development'. Since then, Lev Zaiko, a Soviet Politburo member, was reportedly more outspoken when he visited Addis Abbaba. The prospect of change may not be as unreal as it appeared to be even a few years ago.

The negotiating table provides the only hope for millions of people as a military solution is out of the question. The recent use of napalm and phosphorus bombing by the Ethiopian military is an added and urgent incentive for international action in the interests of both the Eritrean and the Ethiopian people who have tortures enough without the terrible costs and losses of war.

The images of Eritrea remain with me and they are images of hope. In spite of their dreadful privations and the unceasing strains of war, morale is high among this remarkable people. They look forward to regaining control of their capital and the cheery farewell most often heard is 'see you in Asmara on Liberation Day'. I think that all of us who travelled the rugged, bleak terrain and met the people hope to return when that day comes, for it will be the day of peace.

I will make the future.

Glenys Kinnock is a primary school teacher and member of the Council of Management of War on Want. She is married to Neil Kinnock, leader of the Labour Party. Jenny Matthews is a freelance photographer, covering news and development issues. She is a founder member of the London agency Format Photographers and her 1985 exhibition, 'In the Company of Women', has been shown throughout Britain.

If you would like to know more about War on Want's work in Eritrea, please telephone or write to:

Martine Billanou,
War on Want,
35–39 Great Guildford Street,
London SE1 0ES,
telephone 01 620 1111.